# Panic Kit

Laura A. Lionello

**Panic Kit**
©2011 by Laura A. Lionello
Weak Creature Press
First Printing, May 2011

All rights reserved. No part of this book may be used or reproduced in any manner whatsoever without written permission from the author except in the case of brief quotations embodied in critical articles or reviews.

This is a work of poetry. Any resemblance to actual persons, living or deceased, events, or locations is entirely coincidental.

Library of Congress Control Number: 2011927697
ISBN: 978-0-9842424-3-6

Printed in the United States of America.

Cover design: Heather DeSerio, Precision Edge Design LLC.

Cover art: Renee Robbins © reneerobbins.com 2011. All rights reserved.

Interior photographs: Karen Klipowicz

For information on other publications available from Weak Creature Press, please email weakcreature@aol.com.

# Panic Kit

Laura A. Lionello

Weak Creature Press
Los Angeles

# Publication Credits

Acknowledgment is made to the editors of the following publications where the following poems, sometimes in previous versions, were first published:

"Addiction" – Green Room Confessionals 2003
"All Empty" – TWA Penumbra 2008
"Autumn" – Threshold, DePaul University, Vol 17, 1997
"Bitter Coffee" – Portland Review, Vol 47 No 1
"Blue Scissors" – The Blue House, April 2004
"Boys I Like I through III" – The Blue House, June 2004
"Boys I Like IV" – The Blue House, April 2004
"The Caryatid and the Bees" – Poetic Diversity, February 2004
"Corpse Pose" – TWA Penumbra 2004
"Cover the Door" – Portland Review 2000
"Harvest Song" – Poetic Diversity, November 2003
"Homemaker" – The Blue House, February 2004
"Indecision" – TWA Penumbra 2002
"On the Island, Alone on the Edge of a Half-Mile Pier" – TWA Penumbra 2003
"Still Life" – TWA Penumbra 2007

# Contents

### Section I
Sour .................................................................................... 3
Addiction ............................................................................ 4
Cathartic Drive .................................................................. 6
Simple Song ....................................................................... 7
Blue Scissors ...................................................................... 8
Indecision ........................................................................... 9
Horizon ............................................................................. 10
Avocado, Floorboard, and Spider Web ....................... 11
What He Said ................................................................... 13
Homemaker ..................................................................... 15
Boys I Like ........................................................................ 16
On the Island, Alone on the Edge of a Half-Mile Pier 19
God Left Then .................................................................. 21

### Section II
Still Life ............................................................................ 25
Bitter Coffee ..................................................................... 27
Ivy ...................................................................................... 28
The Dream ........................................................................ 29
The Moon Said No .......................................................... 30
All Empty .......................................................................... 31
Harvest Song .................................................................... 32
Skinning the Girl ............................................................. 33
Cover the Door ................................................................ 34
About the Poem You Are Not In .................................. 35
The Moon Isn't Exactly . . . ............................................ 36
Corpse Pose ...................................................................... 37
Garden .............................................................................. 40
Corner Bar ........................................................................ 41
Saturation ......................................................................... 43
Night Song ....................................................................... 44

Six responses to the phrase, "when body and mind collide" ................................................................................... 45

**Section III**
The Other Cat ........................................................................ 51
Moon Again ........................................................................... 52
Autumn .................................................................................. 54
The Extraction ...................................................................... 55
The Caryatid and the Bees ................................................. 56
A bell rang ............................................................................. 57
Morning in Boston, Fall 2004 ............................................ 58
Embroidered ......................................................................... 59
Parking Structure 4, Santa Monica .................................. 60
Little Poem ............................................................................ 61

*For Wayne*

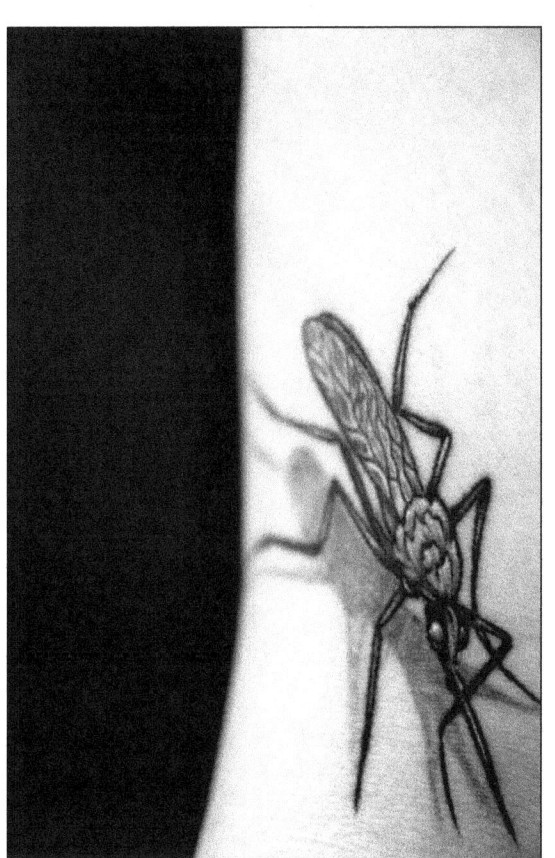

## Sour

Double-jointed broomstick
with elbows and a dust
stare, the man leans over
his knees to tell me
everything. His voice, dry
white noise starching the room:

Time squared, solitude or
new words for solitude
like wanderlust. A bird's
nest filling with water.
Thirteen months away from
home like stations of the cross.

As he speaks, the moon rasps
against the cold bricks and
I think I am going
to suffer for this.
The buzzard in my belly
scavenges and a hard voice
exits my throat, a struggle.

If I were my body, I'd run like hell.

## Addiction
*For Steven*

Addiction is just the search for
permanence and your landlocked
state is no panacea.
You, with your head
hanging
like a loose tooth,
snapped twig, dejected dog.
At eight I saw your feral skull
exposed,
the garish white bottom
of an angel's cauldron
filling with plural red.

I imagine the addiction has been
growling
within you since –
the way a neighbor's fight
is infused into an adjoining wall,
the sadness edges gathering
dust, growing brittle and settled,
biding time.

You take your morning coffee
with cola chasers,
text-message
suicide notes to hours
en route to destinations
in rural Illinois.
You call me with the names of towns,
tell me the prices of cigarettes.
*Yes,* you say. *I'm driving alone.*

I think of what you might look like
shucked or hanged, with only one distracted
leg, a perfect hole in your throat,
or staring neatly
into the bright light of white birthday candles
standing like pointing fingers.
Would you see what I see:
gradient-filled horizons, a touch of absurdity,
regret and regret,
regret.

We grow into our addictions
with the patience of oak trees and rocks.
We throw dry tea leaves at each other,
green with desire.
We stumble into an accidental heaven.
We slowly close our eyes.

## Cathartic Drive

Cathartic drive like the laws of fire
in the dry season, I tilt the right
side-view mirror in to see how I look
driving out of the city. Angled profile,
I'm a brown blood blister with cadaver neck.

Stabbing the night and its kept secret, I
follow you all the way from Morro Bay
to San Francisco. Your backseat is filled
with plaid bedding, shopping bags, fresh produce;
mine is filled with cigarette ash and soul stuff.

I tail you over northbound passes and
downgrades, where our tires roll like promises
the dead made while still alive. The central
coast choke dissipates into Bay Area mist,
washing the putrid angel from my windshield.

Exalted in your ruby sedan, you become my
current god, lacking nothing but tinted windows.
Your pulse pours through my open vents,
cools my dark interior. We overtake each other
a dozen times before hitting the Bay Bridge.

You take the ramp right and pay the toll.
I drive down and into the buckled bay –
a galaxy of headlights between us.

# Simple Song

Warm woman like red
rocks and rusting,
mornings of stretching and mood.
I wake to find furniture
rearranged, vinyl warped,
dust bunnies gnawing at
mattress. This is
simple life
with pencils, dandelion
sprigs, cracked cement.
You and cat sit at window
watching rain fill dip in street.
I move heavy to kitchen.
You and cat pad there, too.
We whistle our little
self-important songs to
dishrag and linoleum.
There is little more than this,
and this:
We kiss and brew coffee,
stronger than you like it but
stronger because I like it.
Sugared and creamed,
coffee cools on your lip.
You lick it away.

## Blue Scissors

Whiskeyed and out of season, I
slither the living room like a
flatfish with flared nostrils. The gauge
barricade of stripped furniture
and moving boxes separates
the yours from the mines and for twenty-
one days I open our door to be
greeted by dust, a fusty mood
rust reminder of what's just junk
now. Today I stand on heroine
toes and secrete a slow motion
on anything not strapped in duct tape.
A filigree of stale smoke stains
the wall in the shape of the Madonna.
I cross myself twice in the hall.

I find a scrap note from you.
The blue scissors are yours,
but they're nestled in a box with the soft
folds of my crocheting and makeup
brushes. Their arms of sharp metal are
syringe placeholders, and sun wedges
through the space in the bent cardboard flaps.
You will get them back, my dear.
On my way out, I will carefully
insert them between your shoulder blades.

## Indecision

I inhale and then go at it
as if nothing in me
is broken. A cracked glass
doorbell glitters in the sun,
as familiar to me as
your chapped hands knuckling and
stretching, knuckling and stretching.
Somehow I'm always better dressed
in memories, where indecision
has a thousand loves and I
love them, too, like I did the boy
who dreamed of climbing mountains
grown never to climb mountains and
my loneliness, which I carry
like a rag doll with one eye.
Don't be alarmed if I'm a
little late. I've been halfway home
for years, but like the way Chicago
forked me into leaving, I'm
tangled in the tines of grass between
me and your door and blue road
rain and the knuckling of your hands
and how the rag doll knew something I didn't.
Or none of this. I step forward, make
my way to your door. My reflection
in the doorbell is reversed, upside down.
I smile like a barren woman and ring.

## Horizon

The stale habit of wanting to be, of wanting
to go. From Chicago in late January
we drove east in silence like empty cups, talking
about times when more important things were more
important, like the stars and white porch lights on the
horizon – one yellow orb lopsided and to
the left, a tiger's eye or another woman's
dream. I was shawled in the dual arch of sky and
the possibility that love is just context
failed, a puddle of ego, admitting a down-
side to depression. Oh, and the moon lounging on
her back in profile, that incidental temptress.

Now all that trying to make sense of what happened.
Now all that trying to make matter what happened.

## Avocado, Floorboard, and Spider Web

I.
The bright orange koi are mired in stasis
and desirability, swarming in the front yard
pond beneath the avocado tree.
On this side of the crisp cedar fence
that separates my yard from the alley,
geometric ivy preens its silk tendrils,
multiplies itself over and over.
Here I'm trapped in the perfect
square of my own redundancy.

II.
For eight days a weak floorboard
in the dining room threatens to
buckle. I keep time with the squeaks as I
pace and sew morphine patches
on my elbows and knees.
My loneliness comes and goes
as it comes and goes, and the dropped
avocado looks like a bald man smiling.

III.
Every third morning I find a spider web
stretched from the kitchen windowsill to the
curved faucet.
I brush it away with the back of my hand,
but every third morning I find it has returned.
It's just one strand, and it glistens
like a baby's mouth.
I think about the web we saw
spanning
from chain-link fence to
stop sign to oak tree to something we couldn't see.

How we crouched and turned around it.
Then, our fingers webbing as we walked home.

## What He Said

I.
He said,
make love with your eyes open, make
war with your eyes closed and now
I can't see for all this theory.
A mine/us, so premeditated.
I'm tapping
my fingers on the table
like a stark –
like a stark indifference.
No, like a stark battle cry
while you rinse out your heart in the kitchen sink.

I'm not going to write a poem about war
any more than I'm going to write a poem
about love.

I'm a serving-sized woman
with the bad smell all over me.
I'm opening my eyes to concern the
self with this slit of moon,
not with its tickles of Indian and ochre
but with its perspective and red tape.
Now I'm only a star to something farther away,
severed and less severe than this crescent moon.

II.
There was a night
seen from a third-story
porch with the sallow sounds of
wind chimes and chained to the laundry line
dogs and the echo of hollow heels on wooden planks.
There was –

There was alley-lamp orange glow,
cell phone you,
moisture and make-believe.
And that was love.

III.
He said, make love with your eyes open,
make love with your eyes, make
love.
And he crawled into my ear canal to whisper:
Lady, you with the tempo of breathing
like the flecks of the moon,
you with the tattooed moth
asleep on your forearms,
when will you decide to start doing things?

# Homemaker

Cavewoman exterior, please pull me
by my hair. I have forgotten about
the use of my plump legs. Take me to your
dark place, lay me on your soft animal
pelt. Lay me close to the dirt, in your filth.

I will peel the smooth skin of your chest like
layers of dry foliage. I will snap
back your crisp twig ribs, bore a hole through your
sternum, and pour myself into the nestle
of your aorta. I will make your heart
my home. I will sweep to the rhythm of
your pulse and dust to your lub-dub, create
homemade dinners of your savory muscle
garnished with a sprig of your white blood cells.

When lonely, I will crawl through your largest
artery to the fat vein on the left
side of your neck that bulges like a snake
digesting when you gulp. I will stretch long,
my arms tickling your chin, my toes stroking
your clavicle. I will let you swallow me whole,
slide me down the clean edge of your trachea,
past the blonde hole in your breast bone and the
messy weeds of your rib cage back to my little red cave.

## Boys I Like

I.
Boys I like collapse and fall from my sight
leaving rust on the trapdoor of the floor and
my lips, two chapped and petty occurrences.
A mess of music seeps through the walls and
curls up on the floor like superstition.
A dragonfly unfurls its wings and the
trapdoor becomes girl talk, a spell book,
kindling. I circle the spot like ring-
around-the-rosy, once for each of them,
until the fire crackles and the ash blinds. In
absence there is chest-tightening and blood
like sweet tea in summer. Broken middle
daughters lost in this resin room. The sound
of dragonfly wings slowly sinks
                                    sinks
                                                            sinks.

II.
They're swarming. Every spring they return like
swallows to the old mission in San Juan
Capristrano. Already their familiar
squawks like a belly itch box my ears and
boys I like are beginning to take flight.
Our coevolution has left me with a
postmarked third eye and lobster claws, left them
sweeter and with dragonfly wings. Up north
they're dragging the lake for the promise keepers
and the stalker who just couldn't leave love
alone. Underripe berries fall like friendship
through holes in the ceiling and there is
a fire storm, chloroformed daughters, and a blocked
trapdoor. I'm in love, but I always leave alone.

III.
You suck
on your cigarette
with the delicacy of a hummingbird.
Your left
index and middle
fingers are Wiccans, mystical guardians
of holy carcinogens. Right hand raised with
match lit
you shake it once, twice,
shake and it is snuffed.
A hedonistic purl of smoke, the duty
of pleasantness and unpleasantness, looks wet.
It takes the soft shape
of the dragonfly and dissipates into
the red sting stinging
your eyes
staring
up at me looking
down at you. I pour
Band-Aids and cabernet
through the oubliette.
Wanting your blood, I had to trap all of you.

IV.
In this room we're broken-
legged and pasted to the center
of the night – a liquid planet and a
searchlight moon. The sound of razorblades
on starlight sinks, sinks,
sinks.

V.
With fire smile all split
lip, a heart burn, dragonfly

fingertips, I reach
for all those mechanical
lovers stuffed under the bed.

## On the Island, Alone on the Edge of a Half-Mile Pier

On the island this morning
the lizards stick themselves to the stucco walls.
Purblind little darlings, they don't peel,
just accept in stillness the thick wind
dripping with knee-jerk anger while cauterized
crabs head for the caves. Between Cayman Brac's
salty breaths, the palm trees stalk motionless
as a child's choir. Chameleon clouds change
color to match the gray-faced palm of the sky and
two black birds with pterodactyl squawk
circle over me on this balcony
as the dark sea exhales a monotone chant.

It's just past hurricane season.
Last night I saw the Southern Cross and
now I'm watching a man
alone on the edge of a half-mile pier
look out past the blue like the sutra
beyond the broken coral reef and the
hapless breakers with the urgency
of the chronically fatigued.
He cranes his neck and I know
he's thinking *out* and *down* –
surface to step, twenty feet.
Step cliff to seabed, four thousand feet.

And at the bottom, there is only water.

Through the grayish-blue plain
I gain courage. More angry
than sad about it, mad girl
I want to tell him to let go or fuck off.

I want to tell him that death in a poem
doesn't have to be cliché, or if it does,
then add the search for sunken treasure
add sophistication and sand castles
add my heart talking to your heart
add God.

*You know,* I want to tell him. *You
could take care of all this for me.*
But I stay silent and he just stares beyond and beyond,
his red jacket moving like flowing blood.

Before the end of this, one of us will have to die.

## God Left Then

Evening crawls between the beige curtain
panels. Lamppost gold glow casts soft,
oblong creatures on the wall, grotesque
but sweet. We fill our pockets with white-
washed beach rocks and hold our hands at prayer
position. Friends come by crying
beautiful about the longing in
their souls, telling stories set against
stony skies, with moon struggle and some
rain absolute and glittering just
like you were that day we sat on the
back deck with green-tinted drinking
glasses, counted the steeples on the
streets below, and then forgot the
final number. I showed you the
honeyed shadow on my heart, caked on
and as yellow as guilt. You shook your
head, laughed, and taught me three new words from
your secret language.
                    God left then,
and we finished our beers just like
that, as though none of us had
anything to apologize for.

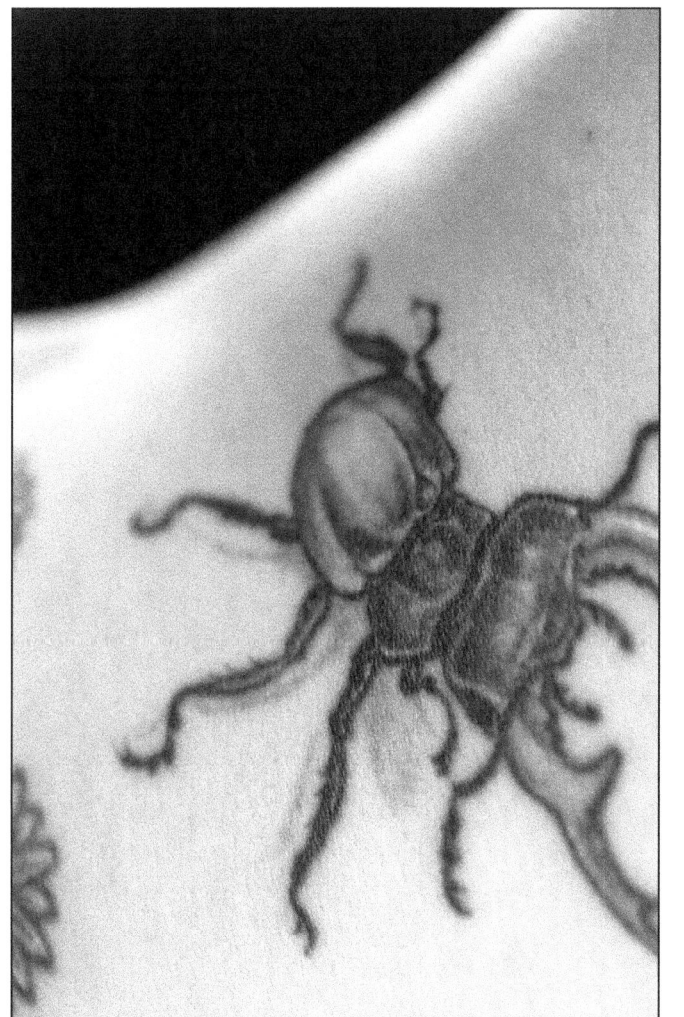

## Still Life

I bought flowers
for the kitchen, daisies and mums
assorted greens
musty and with serrated edges.
I used the everyday vase
and filtered water,
sliced a lemon and packed the disks
among the scraped stems.

Yes, the knife gleamed.
Yes
       it winked casually of the
dissolvable nature of my being,
and this concerned me.
This concerned me more than the bullets
buried in the coffee grounds and the clean
gun nestled between two slices of
sourdough in the breadbox.
              This concerned me
more than the phone calls I'd have to make,
more than the wish that life would have more
meaning for me,
more than all those poems that could only
be written after discovering a truth like this.

And this truth surrounded me.
It surrounded me
and it threatened to swallow me,
its saliva laced with toxins.

I can't really prepare for death,
or maybe I already have,
and although I am not

my ability
to dissolve like an aspirin
in a bucket of fresh cut flowers,
I cling to the idea as though it were my desire
which is also not me.

## Bitter Coffee

Someone's gonna have a lot
of explaining to do: the clocks
pushed back an hour-and-a-half,
three dank knocks resounding
at the back door, the sugar
switched with the salt, and all
this spilled milk.
                    No use in
cleaning it up. The cats will
lap up the rivulets before
it all seeps under the fridge.
Let the rest sour there
as a reminder. Oh I do
know, and thank you – whoever
it was inside me who
compelled me to do it and then
to forget that I did it
to myself – for the reminder
that I'm destined
to misinterpret the signs,
to always run late, to search
again and again for faces
to attach to those voices that whisper
how necessity grows
through my bitter coffee.

## Ivy

I plunge my hands
into the pot of soft dirt to
dig up the root of the dead ivy
and pull out all these mismatched
slices of angel –
real sweet stuff that leaves a glossy
film on my palms.
                     I arrange the slices
on the coffee table in a
confused mosaic: blue eyes
next to wing pieces, lung chunks and
knee caps, an empty sword sheath and a halo.

This is a new kind of mourning,
so I will need blank paper
and peach brandy, something meaningful
to clutch tightly or to burn.
These are my angels,
but I do not recognize them,
their gold pins perforating my chest,
their brass-knuckled winks in my direction:
part bruised pit
part flesh feather.
And I know I don't belong
among these green things and precious things,
more with the mud and the brine,
but I dust the root body
with sugar and cinnamon.
I raise it to my mouth slowly and chew.
And I snarl
bits of ivy matter stuffed between my teeth.

## The Dream

In the dream I wanted a child so badly
that I invented one.
I carried my dummy child up and down the bleached
aisles of the grocery store,
a brunette doll with painted eyes, moving
eyelids, and real lashes. I juggled her flour-sack
body in one arm and the cereal boxes and
soup cans in the other.
But, because I wasn't versed in caring for a child,
I forgot her. I left her in the dairy case
when I picked out the eggs, left her dumb, full diaper
warming the butter and spoiling the yogurt.

The checker in the express lane
wore a green smock and had a soft
pink scar above his left eyebrow.
As he handed me the change
he looked deep into me
where a soft wind fluttered, where
a sea of bile lapped quietly
in my belly
and he knew
I was not a real mother.

Ashamed as a sunburn,
I took my canvas sack and passed
through the automatic door as a long row of carts
as gnarled as the index finger of an old woman
moved in my opposition.

## The Moon Said No

Nighttime is made for women
    who bleed.
When the moon curls its golden fingers
around my neck,
        the black cake of muscle and
        error hardens in my gut.

I stand
    in front of a polished table
    that doesn't talk back
and everything I touch becomes crude,
brown, and outrageous.

When the moon said no,
    it left me starless, one.

Now I incubate under the sun.
My flesh
    cracks and oozes starchy shame.
My hair breaks,
    each strand a hinged spider leg.

My womb is as empty as my hand
reaching out into this warm room.

## All Empty

One winter night in Boston we stood
still on the back porch of my sister's house and
smoked as the black-boned arms of the
hedge maples took us in their grooved embrace.
The sky clear, the stars sharp and hung low.

A kindless bird pealed on about the way
things are done in this type of world, the
type where you don't spend time counting stars
without expecting something from the result.

Maybe there is a god, you said, but that's
not the issue now.
If there, he can't be bothered with failures
like these. There are some losses
you just don't get over.

This is not to say that my pain is
deeper
than your pain.

A pregnancy I terminated: One new body
added to my constellation of errors.
I pry open the bathroom window
from the inside to get to the outside,
cut the screen and crawl out backwards, feet first.
I am fever chart and lipsticked mouth
angry need and sagging belly
empty.

## Harvest Song

A murder of crows lifts its bundled
body from the telephone wire and
moves south. The vibration of the wire
lingers as long as the lighted disk
in full moon phase, and this fall
Sunday boils like a nerve storm.
      Girl without style,
I walk my little
barefoot walk. I walk a tainted
tempered walk, kindled and caught. The
blister on my toe throbs and the sky's
pregnancy wanes. My skin flakes, I grow
horns, and the crows are goblins getting smaller.

Tiny soft bites, the quarreling
marigolds flutter at my bare
ankles. A small god shines there, too.
I know, sustenance is female, but
more and more I learn to live with lack.

## Skinning the Girl

Like a supine serpent with nine
claws, I slithered with palms raised
from the shadow of the ash tree,
my mouth alive with sticky spit.
It was that summer I tried
self-forgiveness instead of
redemption. It was that summer
I walked past you as I shed my
dead layer. Skinned girl, I had to look back.
By that time I was sure I had
lost you in the move, was sure you'd
had enough of it, too. You'd been there
with me, sewn to my quilted guilt,
under the table, behind the
razor wire, down the wishing well
and then up again. And then all
again. And that dry winter night
when I flattened my belly on
the cold dirt and slithered west,
you let me go. I swore to you
that if you came to me again
I would die, and then you did
but I didn't
and now I have to live with that.

## Cover the Door

Hey, I'm choking here. I cover
the door dutifully in water-
soaked rags but I'm not so sure
I don't want to go with him. That
slow smolder, a sure promise for
quiet, feathered death.
                            Ah, but for
the facts. I denied that fiery
path you left. I stayed here with these
dozen or so charred ways I'm still –
for now – your survivor. (By that
I do mean shortchanged.) Death changed
your presentation, I alter
my obsession, and then marvel at the
realization: Those hundreds
of casual ways to say you're dead
are almost sweet. Just soot-stuffed grief.

You're just dust now.

My literal observation,
our simultaneous cremations:
You, weightless gray flecks
of absolution.
Me, a burnt crust. I
am your fortified
daughter. Overcooked. Well-done. Well,
done. If you're finished, I'm done.
Your little unsavory meal.

## About the Poem You Are Not In

I was this hungry once
last year. And you, little
wooden death mask, just chewed.
The bawdy funeral
mass music caught in my ears
like camphor and communion.
I'd run out of others
to blame, was just being
breathed. For months I gathered
like brittle fish bones
all the reasons to stay here,
not to stay here, to eat the earth, to go
hungry.
And then I swallowed and
four more years passed and the wine
hadn't answered and I
somehow wrote a poem
that you weren't in.
                      Now
I am simply missing you
as I often do
especially when drunk or
when early evening slows,
when my hunger stops.

I hope that things by you
are good, or at least okay
enough that you can stop
and notice how the rain
sounds – if it is raining
by you, too.

## The Moon Isn't Exactly . . .

The moon isn't exactly
my enemy
but it'll do for now.
We tell lies about the moon –
that it's new or full,
blue;
that it holds secrets
has magic
we didn't invent for it.
The moon doesn't care.
It dims itself, indifferent.

The most noteworthy thing
I've done in my life is
get over your death.
Now I nest and spend money,
laugh and enjoy sex.
I make plans.
At night I drink red wine and,
sometimes, I don't go outside.
From the perfect square of the bedroom
window I watch those long years of
grief, just the remnants of
burnt-out stars speckled at
impossible distances and that moon,
that flecked fist with protruding knuckles
boned into the crook of God's elbow.

## Corpse Pose

I.
The singular aspen is white
and panicked as a wish. It is
shedding its brittle skin of singed
paper like demon tongues. It is
licking the air like a hungry lover,
like soft tide coming in from the west.

Somewhere a wheezing child
wades barefoot through deaf wires
looking for a skull in the moon.
Somewhere else
a man flushes his identification
down the toilet,
and nearby a woman begins
every third morning
with a promise to abstain.
Cellulose and enlarged pores,
smeared mascara like a battalion,
she is survived by all those things
she has somehow gotten away with.
Sometimes she can't believe
what she's gotten away with.
This isn't now.

II.
You are still gone
and I
am becoming aware of my belly,
how it rises and falls,
how it is becoming more elastic and supple.

There is so much silence

between these breaths that come
without expectation.

I am apt to let this continue.

III.
I am a preserved
piece of birch wood, burnt out
and carefully watching
the city's gray outline through
the smudged dining room window.

I don't have to be
right all the time, but it helps –
especially when
deciding which shoes I'll wear
the next time I visit you.

When wrong, I cower
behind the houseplants and it
snows. I palpitate
with the drop of each flake and
nourish the ferns with my sweat.

IV.
Look, you're still gone.

V.
I am petrified
like even-tempered boredom.
A perfectly transfixed panic kit,
I have eyes on each of my fingertips.

Starched voices love valium,
insomnia enhances lithium's parched

stare at all those antidepressants
that adore a good merlot.
Dumb medicine, dumb head,
I leave a worried tread
from the desk to the bathroom, from the
bathroom to the desk, from the desk . . .

VI.
The soul is a bridge to desire
spanning ever more treacherous
currents of memory that
I don't even benefit from anymore
and it begins
with my interminable heartbeat
throbbing in my warm ears
and pouring out my open palms.

Look, I'm still breathing.

## Garden

The trouble you promised never
materialized and now I'm
left alone in the Japanese
Friendship Garden with a half-
empty bottle of SoBe.

Green and yellow moss bond like
putty across the pond but
it's too bright here and
I'm sliding.
My toes touch the water and I
hate myself just a little bit for it.

Trust is not a color
but the pink lotuses promise
redemption and amnesia,
their long stalks pesky with dew.

Not everything is something to
write a poem about
but when you said our instinct is
always first to jump
my bones bleached and the search parties
came in for good.

The devil is a mouth.

## Corner Bar

I wake early to the dark, wet hours.
My heart breaks in half
and then in half,
so I make coffee and sweep the hall.
The city sighs quietly with the
cement virgin under the overpass
while smoke from the burning
garbage in my chest stains my lungs
and burns my eyes.
The last of the lingering stars
rubs its eyes in disinterest
and turns away from the coming day.

The neighborhood stays damp all morning,
stymied in humidity and phlegm.
With death rattle posture
I search for exposed invisibility,
the ability to touch everything
and not leave a fingerprint.
But I've been tripping wires
all over town and my presence
here is widely known.
So now I'm bawling between the
beer taps in the corner bar again.
Maybe I could wave like the wildflowers
among the starchy grasses on the lakeshore;
I would molt if I had to
and go dormant after the first frost.
But I don't spore or speak,
just smoke and smell of yellowed sleep.
And with these bowels of a rat,
this skin of a snake,
I might one day become prey to the jackals

that are beginning to haunt the edges of my secrets.

No one is going to save me from this,
my mutilated perception and mulch-filled need,
the possibility all around me.

# Saturation

*For Karen*

Composed and slipping off my shoes
I step gently from the pier as the
shrouded mountain folds edgeless into
the sea. The dusk sighs its
dirty breath, holds a holy ghost
in its palms. Gulls scavenge on cracked
shells in tangled kelp. I read wide
the timeless language of the sand
and the six-sided sky comes closer
to my bent head – enchanting, not
like the bones of angels. Not like me.

Black on blackening, the mountain looks
disappointing and regards me with
disdain – a weak heretic, sorry
soul. The orange moon is a puncture
wound. This sky I watch is
saturated and sad, swollen
with palsied prophets and black bells.

In my dreams, I sometimes have my
sister's faith and from East Coast to
West Coast, our hands are touching.

## Night Song

Night is poorly drawn around the city.
It misses the bleached spots on the freeway
and the mud-raised outlines of my footprints.

The moon has a toe and haunted marrow,
small-hour comfort to be scratched. The sky
invents fever blisters and sticky stars.

The whip-stitched panic of birds caterwauls
with the uterine secretions of the streetlights
and the windy room of my bloody parts.

Tonight, death imagines me in her bed.

## Six responses to the phrase, "when body and mind collide"

I.
Tulips with their heavy heads
bow to my humility and
the pavement beneath me
becomes a field of pitchforks.
I walk through the neighborhood
tasting blood in my cheek and
with the quiet need that punctures
the soles of my feet. Sometimes
I come to doors I was once
invited to pass through
and then move on.

II.
My cat is the saint of early-
morning noises. When I pad
bare-toed across the smooth hardwood
he warns, *Watch your step. I have
not yet retracted my claws.*
He wants his kibble.
I, my coffee.
In nourishment, we both fall
into our stomachs and churn.

III.
Your heart is a bright plot of grass
at the end of a gangway. In your soil
readies an army of familial
assassins. Through the dark halls
of hunger you devour
morsels of memory as though
they were the glowing words that

hover in 2 AM stillness
like unclaimed stars and, no wonder,
you can't collect them fast enough.

IV.
Sighs the heart in the elephant
graveyard of a lonely woman's chest,
"The mind lies
but the body speaks truth."

V.
I'll be sad again,
eventually, so I say to him
*none, I guess.* None to
God and his thick brown shade,
the dark thing that scratches
at the sole of the foot, the
gnawing in the gut, and all those
stars, stars, stars
impossible to know
my expectancy.
None, I guess.

VI.
This is no way to pray.

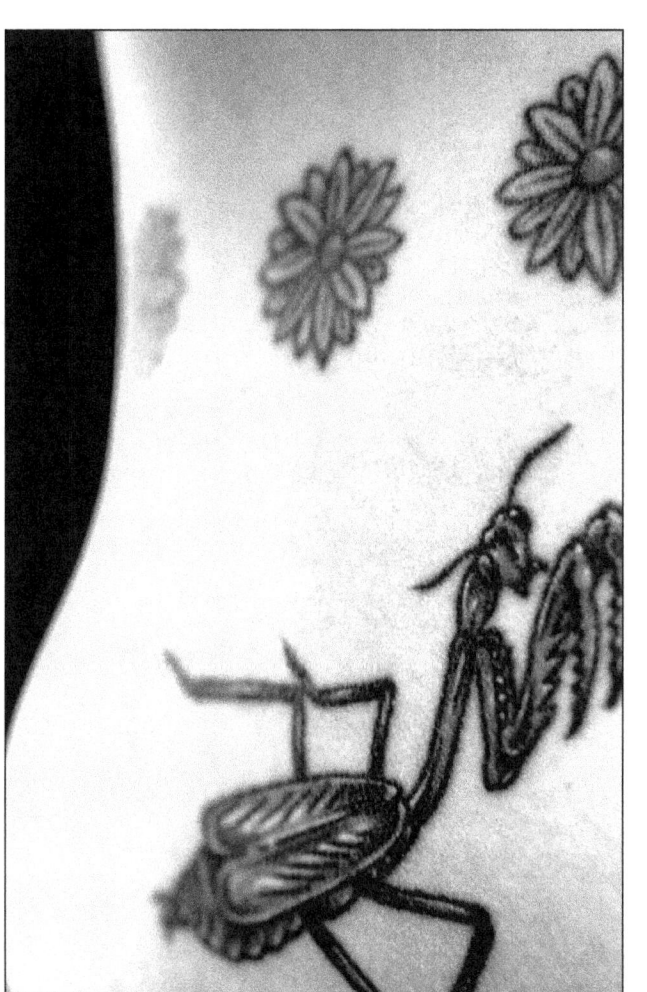

## The Other Cat

All of my stars hanging out and a
moon shape beating through my chest, I
twitch with the tick of the clock, that
nervous gray finch in the corner,
not dozing, not powerful, just
thin and imperfect
time like a
wall cloud, like thundersnow, like
passive disappointment. Time is
a complicated companion.
Remember that time we drank
until we could peer down the clear
glass throats of the wine bottles
at the wet reflections of our third eyes?
You wished for wings,
and I told you that I didn't think
I truly loved the other cat.
You said there's always an other,
brought me to the brown leather chair to
sit it out.
Not so gently, you tugged my hair
at the root, promised that hell is
knowing what you're waiting for.

## Moon Again
*For BBGS*

Moon again,
this one swaying, made of wood
and stone. The door half-open,
the moon descended, made its
way into my room, and took its
place among the others.
Spoiled for choice, I thumbed my
moon treasures, those survivors
of all my sorrows and longings.
Heart like a cataract, tongue foggy
with thirst, fingernails
split from all the moon work, I
sat star-angry and mouthing nails.

Behind me, the Grim Reaper
tapped on my shoulder for a
half hour. He said, begin by
gathering supplies. I reached
for a pen,
two bottles of water,
a grenade,
your hand.

We followed the fog blindly
along the cloud base, its
soggy chest swelling
with the wind shear. Planes were going
down, the echoes of souls tugged
at our earlobes. We ran. Our
bellies empty, the water
running low, our bare heels about

to burst with blood.
And from behind the gray film
above us, another new moon
began to raise its eyelid.

## Autumn

Sitting on the bank of the crooked lake
drowsy and drizzling sand speckles
on the leaves of marigolds, thinking
they are gorgeous in their crinkled orange marsh

sweetness, thinking about looking at things
differently, they are thinking that they
have never been here before. All day
wafting in and out of the green grass swamp

plumpness, eating the spicy sun
knots, drinking the blue-gray gush of the lake,
pushing back the breeze with their starched stems,
speaking through the red buds of their bellies.

In the dark velvet waters that melt by
there floats this wispy pear bloom, streaming the
channels, sniffing loose green amaryllis leaves.

## The Extraction

What a jolt.
This sledgehammer pounding
away at my nailhead tooth.
The gloss all
shattered
save one diamond dunt,
a glint as in a pupil.
My cavity bores
all the way down to the nerve.
The roots of my wisdom tooth
are false tails.
They will have to pull it.

Needle sweet, that
Novocain treat.
My wolf lung swells
at oncoming pliers.

The extraction complete,
I am one
member fewer.
The blood moat in my jaw
is being sopped up with gauze.
The sutures are pulled tight,
and so with decay removed,
I am made right.

## The Caryatid and the Bees

She stands hammertoed and squat
as a bulldog. Baring her teeth to her weight-
bearing function, she spreads her shoulder
blades and emits blue breath through a
limestone throat. Soft bell, her smooth
hair done up in a hive is flattened by the
honeycombed platform she balances.
She is oblivious to the flesh-shy swarm
salivating between her toes, worshiping
her calcified soul like lame props while
her hands wrap gently around her porous
ankles, ghost orchids in a wet forest.
Now she stretches spine to crown, spine to pubis.
The sharp tongues of bees jab at her ears,
slurp at her breast, and suck at her navel.
Their feverish feet leave tacky tracks
along her wrists and inner thighs.
In her new and elegant upright pose,
she yields lime and does pride like a river.

For every one queen, there are sixty-five drones.

## A bell rang

on the day that heaven
tore its seam from the earth.
Someone cried out
        in a room full of people.
Some grass turned green,
        some yellow or brown.
The ocean flexed a muscle. And I
finished carrying packages into the kitchen.

## Morning in Boston, Fall 2004

Because the palm leads to the
heart
I stretch and press mine
flat against the cold glass of the rear
passenger-side window.
Up front, a sour mouth
does the heart's work on another
forming a long line of vibration
and fit.
The car emits ether from its tailpipe,
aromatic puffs of burning
malaise floating from the turnpike and
dotting the infesting suburbs and their
couched confusion.
All across New England,
things
are coming to the heart.
Bare trees stand
like accusations, hours burn, the air goes dry.
I watch with stone eyes
crammed
into their sockets, with
concrete hands dropping lame into my lap
as Boston folds in and out of malignancy.

## Embroidered

When pleated, I can fold into the thinnest
slits. Garment without zippers, backed with basting,
smooth thread. To my hems tatted lace covers knit-
stitched skin. Fabric-covered buttons dot my
cloth in paisley smears.
                    I imagine myself
the patterned product of a great seamstress: full-
length gown born of deft hands adorning like
camisoles slim, white bodices.
                    Instead, my size
has been mismeasured and I am of no use.
Ill-proportioned fit, I hang in the closet
bulky and bulged as an overcoat.

## Parking Structure 4, Santa Monica
is all slant and piss.
The residue of rubber on the
curved turning walls seems to
pout like a pretty girl
alone in a bar with music.
Concrete is golden
height and width in perfect proportion,
an offering to the holy
fluorescents that wash
the walls of the elevator.
The light slides itself translucent
under the gums, hums
*Yes, I'm still lonely*
*Etcetera.*
        *Etcetera.*
Its effects are undetectable
and irreversible.

This whole place was built to be
forgotten the moment you pay
for the privilege of leaving,
but at the top the air clears.
Georgian Hotel, rooftop first
and then the rest,
the nativity and even Venice,
grow into sunset and pier.
Pacific like a prayer seems to say
*I'm like you, only beautiful.*

## Little Poem
*After Bukowski*

There's a woman in my gut
who wants to get out
but I'm too stubborn for her.
I say, not a chance, babe.
I'm not going to risk
being empty in there, too.

# Acknowledgments

Thank you, first and always, to my husband and best friend, Wayne; and to my family, those who are here and those who are no longer; and to the many friends who have seen me through this and other tragedies.

Thank you to all who have read, listened to, and shown interest in my poetry.

Special thanks to Douglas Richardson and Jen Cairns at Weak Creature Press, and Heather DeSerio at Precision Edge Design LLC. And I will forever be indebted to Renee Robbins for providing the stunning cover art and to Karen Klipowicz for taking those fabulous photographs of me. And finally, I am thankful to Michael Smolarek for his careful eye and insistence that I title my poems.

# About the Author

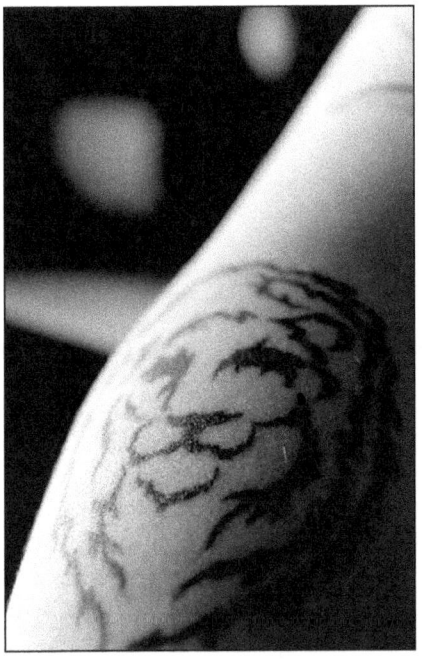

Laura A. Lionello was born in 1975 and raised in the Chicagoland area. She earned her bachelor's degree in English Literature from DePaul University in 1997. From 1999 to 2004, she lived in various cities in Colorado and California, working and writing poetry. Her poetry has appeared in numerous publications, both in print and online. She is currently the managing editor for an educational publisher. Laura lives atop the Logan Square neighborhood of Chicago with her husband, Wayne.

## Also by Weak Creature Press:

*Poems for Loners* by Douglas Richardson
In his fourth enigmatic offering, Douglas Richardson employs poems, lyrics, proverbs, letters, and a diary to illuminate the dark lives of loners.
**ISBN-10:** 0984242422 (paper)
**ISBN-13:** 978-0-9842424-2-9 (paper)

*The Corruption of Zachary R.* by Douglas Richardson
Compunction and collusion drive Zachary R. He harbors disillusionment even while performing life's richest rituals: employment, courtship, marriage, and fatherhood. Memories of a neurotic mother and emotionally austere father shade his adult life with ever-darkening tones. Riddled with madness, he reaches out to those who survive him, those whom he loves, those who will seek to do him harm. Their collective path to sanity is neither uncomplicated nor without redemption. Who among them will survive the journey?
**ISBN-10:** 0984242414 (paper)
**ISBN-13:** 978-0-9842424-1-2 (paper)

*Out in the Cold, Cold Day* by Douglas Richardson
Poetry chapbook offered exclusively through the publisher. (paper)

All titles offered by Weak Creature Press may be purchased directly from the publisher. Please send an e-mail to **weakcreature@aol.com** for orders or inquiries. Otherwise, you may purchase our titles via online retailers or ask your local bookseller to order them for you.

www.ingramcontent.com/pod-product-compliance
Lightning Source LLC
LaVergne TN
LVHW051156080426
835508LV00021B/2655